THE
Archive Photographs
SERIES

AROUND
BATLEY

Batley Coat of Arms, on a postcard, c. 1905. The town's former industries are indicated by the fleece and sheaf. Stars (mullets) are frequently found as heraldic symbols. The cross relates to the old Batley family of Copleys. The motto translates to 'Let (or may) industry flourish.'

THE
Archive Photographs
SERIES

AROUND
BATLEY

Compiled by
Norman Ellis

CHALFORD

First published 1996
Copyright © Norman Ellis, 1996

The Chalford Publishing Company
St Mary's Mill, Chalford,
Stroud, Gloucestershire, GL6 8NX

ISBN 0 7524 0374 5

Typesetting and origination by
The Chalford Publishing Company
Printed in Great Britain by
Redwood Books, Trowbridge

Contents

Acknowledgements

The author appreciates the valuable help given by many people
in the preparation of this book.

Thanks to the staff of Huddersfield Local History Library.

Thanks to Mrs J.T. Foggo of Dewsbury, Mrs W. Greenwood of Batley Carr and Rosalind Stead
of Dewsbury. Also to Bob Burrows for permission to use pictures of Carlinghow Mills.
Useful information comes from back issues of the *Batley News*.

The book relies heavily on postcard photographers/publishers. Two of them, who recorded the
passing scene during the first decades of this century, and whose work features significantly in
this book, deserve mention. James Glen of Henrietta Street, Batley, produced many fine
images of the town. Fred Hartley of Dewsbury was a prolific photographer and postcard
publisher in his home town. His work extended to Batley Carr and Hanging Heaton.
Fred Hartley was the grandfather of Rex P. Hartley, who still lives in the area.

Introduction

Over a century ago, Bill Hanson was the dyer at Old Mill in Batley. One day, the mill chimney was blown down. It distributed copious amounts of soot into the open dye pans and changed the colour of the soaking cloth. Bill assumed that the pieces of spoiled cloth would be unsaleable, but the opposite was the case. More pieces of the same kind were required. Customers were advised by circular that this was nigh impossible because of the difficulty of persuading old mill chimneys, with the requisite amount of soot, to collapse at the right time.

Milltown Batley was blessed with plenty of lofty chimneys, which were supposed to carry the smoke and fumes away. The effect of these products on a neighbourhood was influenced by the height of the chimney. A low chimney discharged smoke into an atmosphere where the prevailing wind stream was disturbed by the mill buildings, and fell to the ground in the lee of them, perhaps enveloping a row of houses.

Every mill (except water-powered) possessed at least one chimney to disperse smoke from the furnace. The latter heated the huge water boiler which produced steam to drive the engine.

Chimneys, like mills, were built of whatever stone was readily available, or alternatively of brick. In the Batley area, stone was widely, but not exclusively, used for mills and chimneys. In general, square chimneys pre-dated round ones.

Most chimneys had three distinct parts: the pedestal at the base; the barrel; and the sills. The pedestal, often square, served as a foundation for the rest of the structure. The sides of the barrel, or main part of the chimney, always tapered towards the top. The barrel invariably had a double wall. At the top were the sills or other forms of decoration, such as panelling or blind arches.

The smoky effluent from a hundred mill chimneys and the thousands of domestic flues turned the town's buff sandstone buildings almost black. Less obvious was the health hazard. The grime was tolerated if not condoned because, to quote an old saying, 'Where there's muck there's money.'

Outbursts of dissatisfaction sometimes occurred. For example, at a meeting of Batley Town Council in July 1906, the Mayor, Alderman George Hirst, complained about the smoke nuisance in the town and said that, if offenders did not mend their ways, the committee would be bound to prosecute. He continued, 'If some offenders would use more coal and less dirt, there would be a great improvement in the atmosphere of the town.'

In the Domesday Book of 1066. Batley received a mention (as Bateleia). When mapped in 1777, Batley was smaller than Birstall, and claimed little more than a church, a few cottages along today's Commercial Street, and separate hamlets such as Batley Carr and Carlinghow. By then, handloom weaving supported much of the population.

By the beginning of the nineteenth century, a few mills had been erected and some mechanisation had been introduced. Coal was mined from day holes and later from deeper mines with vertical shafts.

In Batley, around 1813, a system, generally attributed to Benjamin Law and Benjamin Parr, was perfected for processing woollen rags. The technique enabled waste woollen material to be broken down to a fibrous state and worked with virgin wool to make a course cloth known as shoddy. Twenty years later, a similar technique was used to produce mungo, a slightly better quality cloth which included reworked harder rags and worsted.

The boom in production of shoddy and mungo happened very quickly. From a handful of mills in 1821 and a population of 3,700, Batley had eighty firms involved in the shoddy and mungo trade by 1860 and a population of 12,000. Such was the impact that, in 1860, 'The History of the Shoddy Trade' by Samuel Jubb was issued by a consortium of printers and publishers, which included Fearnsides of Batley.

Vast quantities of rags began to arrive at the railway stations in Batley and Dewsbury from London and provincial towns, Scotland, Ireland, Europe, America and Australia. The rags were auctioned at Dewsbury and Batley Stations, chiefly the latter. In time, most of the rag sales were transferred to properly adapted premises established by Dewsbury auctioneers. Street rag-and-bone men were a clear reminder of a great industry.

Samuel Jubb recorded some interesting facts and figures in his book. In 1858, Batley had 500 female rag sorters, with 40 foremen overseeing them. The women earned between 6s 6d and 7s per week; the foreman 20s to 25s. There were 1,260 hand-loom weavers and 500 power-loom weavers. The latter, whose numbers were increasing, were generally women, earning around 10s per week. They were supervised by men called tuners.

Jubb recorded that Batley's textile trade employed about 900 boys and girls, some of whom still spent half their time at school. The poorest paid received 1s 9d per week. Jubb wrote, 'The closing of mills at two o'clock on the Saturday afternoon, affording as it does nearly a half day holiday, is no doubt regarded as a great boon to the operatives.'

Between 1850 and 1870, a considerable amount of building took place in Batley, when the town which is familiar today began to take shape. Large numbers of workers' houses were built in several areas, including what became the town's central zone. The activity was accompanied by a surge in church and particularly chapel building. The Mechanics' Institute (later adapted as the Town Hall) was erected in 1853. Batley became a borough in 1868.

The initial boom was short-lived. The techniques which started in Batley were appropriated in other countries, which led to a decline in availability of waste material. Failure to invest in advancing technology, fierce competition between mills, and small profit margins were further contributory factors. Batley had become a town largely dependent on one type of industry.

Following a period of relative stagnation in the mungo and shoddy trade, Batley experienced a further intensification of activity in the first part of the twentieth century. The Boer and First World Wars created a huge demand for military overcoats. By adopting updated techniques and using new railway links, the second boom lasted, with minor fluctuations, until the 1930s. Loss of jobs was partially halted by the introduction of the carpet industry to the town in 1938.

Today's national waste recycling is nothing new; Batley was in the business 150 years ago. The mill chimneys were once likened to the stems and flower heads of plants trying to find the light. Their disappearance is sadly a sign that the town's once great textile industry is little more than a memory.

Many of Batley's mills were soundly and solidly built, with appealing architectural features. Some of them have been demolished; others, partly through the help of government grants, have been restored for alternative and sometimes textile related use. Consequent to the rise of the town's textile-industry was the formation of the Market Place. It is Batley's jewel.

One
Town and Around

Batley from the north, *c.* 1910. The tower of the Public Library which overlooks the Market Place, is visible to the right of the centre.

Commercial Street, 1904, taken from near the junction with Hick Lane. The elegant Wilton Arms, where Batley Town Council used to meet, is on the right.

Commercial Street, c. 1910, viewed from a similar spot to the upper picture. Children cluster outside the shops of Fred Brearey, pork butcher, and Miss Cook, draper and milliner.

Commercial Street, late 1905. George Parrot's wholesale and retail butchering establishment is on the left. Beyond Crown Street is the shop of J.W. Smith, watchmaker, jeweller and optician (with clock). The same block of buildings contained a pawnbroker and the Crown Hotel.

Commercial Street, c. 1912. Amongst various shops are two well known printing establishments – J.S. Newsome, with the tall pointed façade, and James Fearnsides, beyond. The Co-op stands in the centre distance.

Commercial Street. Many of the jobs created in Batley's new mills were filled by immigrants, including a significant influx of Irish workers. The town's population more than trebled between 1820 and 1860. This period of growth led to an escalation in trading facilities and house building. In the 1850s, some jumbled housing in Commercial Street, then a rutted lane, was converted into shops. By the 1870s, older buildings were being demolished to make way for new shops with living quarters above. Commercial Street became the main shopping thoroughfare. Along it in 1912 were around two dozen butchers, a dozen grocers, a similar number of milliners and drapers, and seven or eight boot and shoe makers. Add to these the fruiterers, fish and poultry dealers, tripe dealers, bakers and confectioners, glass and china shops, ironmongers, furnishers, clothiers, saddlers, tobacconists, and newsagents. The street had four chemists; working-class people preferred the relatively cheap self-medication from the apothecary rather than a doctor's hefty bill. Commercial Street was a favourite contender for decorations to suit special occasions. The floral arch was erected for the July 1905 celebrations, which included the opening of the Town Hall.

Commercial Street, c. 1912, with the magnificent minareted Batley Co-operative Society building. The shops on the left include three famous names – Maypole Dairy, Altham Ltd and Taylor's Drug Co.

Commercial Street, late 1930s, after the then recent road widening on the left. This necessitated the demolition and replacement of many properties. Observe the new concrete lamp standard near the end of Crown Street.

Market Place, looking towards Upper Commercial Street, c. 1905. Yorkshire Woollen District tramcar No. 36 stands at the terminus, whilst a Great Northern Railway rulley stops to deliver goods to one of the shops.

Market Place and Upper Commercial Street, late 1930s. The entry to Branch Road is on the right. Vero's shop on the previous view underwent a change of ownership c. 1930, when it became part of the Greenwood conglomerate, which specialised in men's wear.

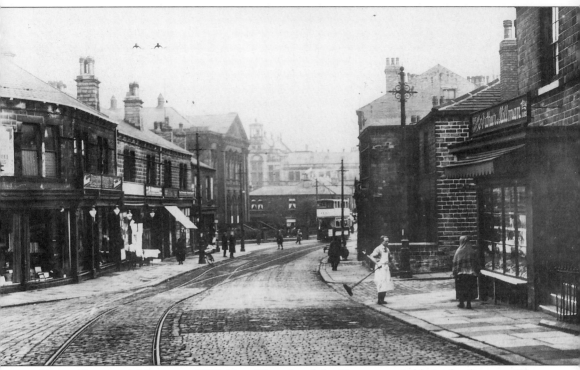

Upper Commercial Street, *c*. 1920. Zion Chapel and the Co-op are visible in the distance. The trams, having run along Mayman Lane and Upper Commercial Street, terminated near the front of Zion, opposite the Market Square. Arthur Millmans's butchering shop is on the right. His other shop was in Cross Bank Road.

Upper Commercial Street, *c*. 1920. This is the same piece of road as that shown in the upper view, but looking in the opposite direction. One of Albert Skidmore's bootmaking and cobblering shops can be seen.

Market Square, looking north, 1904. Around the square and the large area which runs up to Wellington Street, sometimes collectively referred to as Market Place, were built many of Batley's finest civic and public buildings. They sharply contrasted with the even bigger mills which dominated some parts of the town. The hillside site, which used to be a cornfield, must have caused some problems to planners and weary pedestrians. The stone setts in this view were laid in 1896. By the side of Zion Methodist Chapel, right, Branch Road descends into the centre distance. If Snowden's sign is any criterion, clearance sales of clothing are nothing new.

Market Place, snow scene, early 1900s.

Market Square, probably 1933. In the foreground is a Leyland centre-entrance bus, new in 1932, of Yorkshire Woollen District Transport. To the right is a London, Midland & Scottish Railway horse-drawn rulley.

Market Square and Town Hall, 1930s. The spire of Hanover Street Congregational Chapel is visible behind. This building, with 600 sittings, was opened on 4 March 1857. It became known colloquially as 't' Pinnacle chapel' because of its tall and graceful spire. It replaced an earlier building in Wellington Street.

Market Hall. This was erected at the top of Market Hill in 1878. It housed twenty-eight stalls and six butcher's shops, as well as various offices, including the borough surveyor's office and a weights and measures department.

Market Hall. Within twenty years, the Gothic-styled building was considered a failure, because many traders preferred to stand outside in fine weather. The hall was demolished, although the tower, with its four-faced chiming clock, survived a few years longer, as pictured.

Market Place. At joint ceremonies on Tuesday 18 July 1905, crowds witnessed the opening of the enlarged Town Hall, and laying the foundation stone for the Public Library. Both events are depicted on one postcard above. The upper view shows the Mayor, Alderman George Hirst, unlocking the door of the Town Hall. The lower one shows the library stonelaying, which immediately preceded the Town Hall opening. In the background is the Independent Methodist Chapel. The foundation stone for this building, which replaced an earlier chapel on the same site, was laid on 14 July 1883. It opened for worship on 1 May 1884. Seating was provided for 350 worshippers; underneath was a Sunday School.

Town Hall reopening, 18 July 1905. The Mechanics' Institute was erected in 1853 by public subscription. It was situated at the side of a field which later became the Market Square, although the main entrance faced Commercial Street. It housed a library, provided classes in reading, writing and arithmetic, and was a meeting place for art and musical groups. After the classes declined, the building was purchased for £3,400 by the Corporation to serve as the Town Hall. By the end of the century, it was considered to be too small. Plans were produced for a new structure which resembled a scaled-down version of Leeds Town Hall. It was to be built on the site of the Market Hall. The cost of erection was estimated at £40,000 and, due to other commitments, a rate rise seemed inevitable. Meanwhile, the existing Town Hall was severely damaged by fire. The cost of its rebuilding, with an extension, was put at £10,000. The councillors opted for a reconstruction of the old building rather than a complete new one. In this picture of the reopening ceremony, the new part of the building, and its new entrance on to the Market Square, are depicted. At the doorway are Alderman George Hirst, Mayor, and Alderman J.W. Turner, chairman of the Town Hall committee.

Town Hall, pavement laying, probably 1905.

Town Hall and Police Station, probably 1927. This was the year when the latter building was erected. At inception, the Police Station had a complement of thirty-six men of all ranks.

Public Library stonelaying ceremony, 18 July 1905. Platforms have been erected for dignitaries and wives. Partly-built walls are visible. The actual memorial stone is on the left.

Library stonelaying. The Mayor, having ceremoniously manoeuvred the memorial stone into position (with some assistance), stands proudly beside it. Copies of various local and national newspapers were placed beneath it.

Public Library and War Memorial, c. 1932.
The latter was erected in memory of soldiers
who fell in the First World War.

War Memorial. It was unveiled by General
Sir Ian Hamilton in 1923. The memorial and
surrounding gardens were laid out on the site
of the Market Hall. Visible in the
background are the swimming baths which
were opened in 1893. Swimming, slipper and
Turkish baths were incorporated; also a
washhouse with drying and mangling rooms.

Public Library and General Post Office, *c.* 1910.

General Post Office, 1906. The building was opened in July 1906, and extended in 1927 to accommodate the telephone exchange.

Branch Road, looking towards the Town Hall, *c.* 1906. The name was adopted because the road branched from Bradford Road. Stott's musical warehouse is on the left. They made pianos and were in business until the mid 1920s. S.T. Church next door (with the Perth Dye Works sign) was a ladies' outfitter.

Branch Road. The arch and decorations were put up for the July 1905 celebrations, which included the Public Library stonelaying and the Town Hall reopening.

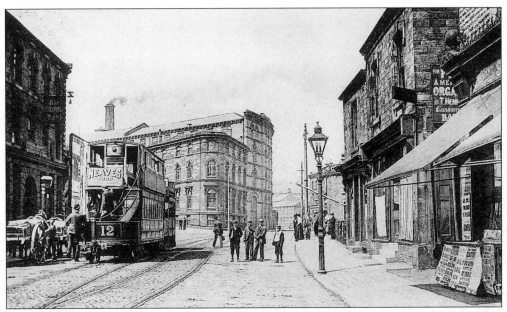

Bradford Road and (behind tram) Hick Lane, probably early 1905. The steam tram and trailer, on a passing loop, are heading in the Birstall direction. Top deck seating ran along the full length of the trailer, facing outwards, similar to a knifeboard, which explains the need for two doors at each end of the deck. This picture comes from a card purchased at Sarah Shaw's newsagency, right.

Blakeridge Lane and Blakeridge Mills, c. 1928. The tramlines curve into Mayman Lane, left. Stocks Lane is on the right. Note the washing.

Cemetery, looking towards the Cemetery Road entrance and Blakeridge Mills, 1905. The 19 acres burial ground was laid out in 1865. Two Gothic-style mortuary chapels and a lodge were incorporated; the latter is on the left, near the entrance. The cemetery was administered by a burial board until transferred to the Corporation, following the 1894 Local Government Act. Attitudes towards funerals have changed considerably during the last few decades. Even working-class families tried to ensure that a deceased relative was given a good send-off. At home, front curtains or blinds were drawn until after the burial. Black outfits, with purple trimmings, were purchased or brought out of mothballs, and worn for weeks afterwards. With undertaker's fees and ham teas, costs were high. Many people had prudently taken out insurance. The grave was later provided with a large headstone, edge stones and possibly chippings. Only the rich afforded the more elaborate monuments, some of which are shown here. Tidiness certainly prevails.

Benny Parr Wood and Lower Mill, Howley, *c.* 1908. The name was adopted locally from Benjamin Parr who, with Benjamin Law, produced shoddy at the small mill.

Carlinghow Old Hall, Ealand Road, 1908. The original hall, built in 1521, had twenty-five apartments and oak panelling. Much of it was demolished in 1800. By the time this photograph was taken, the remains were in a sorry plight, but some of them lasted until 1969.

Track Road, looking north, *c.* 1913. On the left are several recently built and fashionable private houses. More houses were erected to their rear in the former grounds of Carlton Lodge. Although double track was laid for the electric trams on the Bradford and Halifax Roads, single track predominated in the suburbs and residential areas, such as here.

Purlwell Lane, *c.* 1912. Purlwell Council School is on the right, behind the trees. This was opened by Batley School Board in 1874.

Lady Ann Road, *c.* 1903. The ruins of Howley Hall are visible on the horizon.

Farfield Nursery and its greenhouses, *c.* 1910. Nearby, the Great Northern Railway crosses the London & North Western Railway. A footpath at the other side of the row of houses, left, leads up to Lady Ann Crossing. St Thomas's Church is on the skyline.

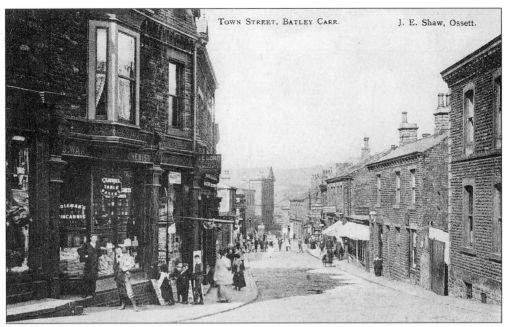

Town Street from Upper Road, Batley Carr, *c.* 1908. The Wesleyan Methodist Chapel, at the corner with Warwick Road, is in the distance.

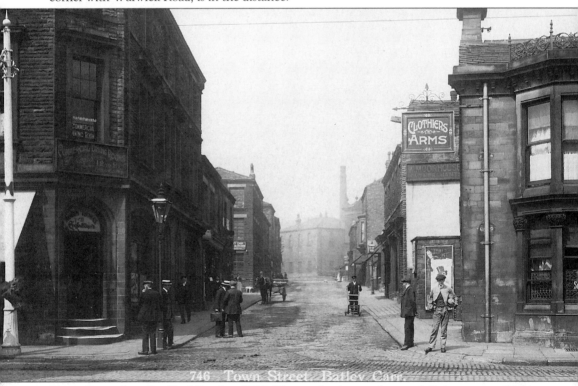

Town Street from Bradford Road, *c.* 1920. The confectionery shop and dining rooms of Misses Thomas are on the left hand corner. The shop was well patronised by millworkers for takeaway meals. The austere looking building in the distance is the Wesleyan Methodist Sunday School.

Old Shoulder of Mutton, Halifax Road, *c.* 1908. Its right hand but sealed-up doorway may once have been the entrance to a butcher's shop. One tram conductor usually called out, 'Healds Road and Shoulder' at the approach to the stop.

Four Lane Ends, Staincliffe, *c.* 1914. The post office is on the corner, right. Christ Church stands in Staincliffe Hall Road.

Soothill Lane, Lower Soothill, looking towards the junction with Oaks Road, *c.* 1908. Clutton Street is in the middle distance, left, near the lamp post.

Soothill Lane, from near Soothill Manor, looking towards Woodkirk, *c.* 1925. John Wilson, who published this card, managed the stationery shop and post office at 49 Soothill Lane.

General View.

W. H. Mitc[hell]
P.O. Hanging Hea[ton]

Hanging Heaton (Upper Soothill), *c.* 1925. Soothill was a large and scattered township. After the Local Government Act of 1894, it was split to form Lower Soothill, Upper Soothill and Nether Soothill. The two latter are now better known as Hanging Heaton and Earlsheaton (their former ecclesiastical names). Under the Batley Extension Order of 1909, the largest part of Hanging Heaton was annexed to Batley. The remainder was joined to Dewsbury, along with Earlsheaton. Hanging Heaton became a self-contained community, with its own church, chapels, schools, shops and post office. This photograph shows St Paul's Parish Church in the distance. Ebenezer United Methodist (formerly Methodist New Connection) Chapel, which was built in 1878, stands on High Street, to the left. The Wesleyan Chapel in Bromley Street was erected in 1887. High Street (mixed) School was built in 1843; Mill Lane (mixed and infants) School was erected in 1874.

High Street, Hanging Heaton, looking west, *c.* 1925. On the left is the United Methodist Chapel. William Henry Mitchell's grocery shop and post office is on the right. Beyond it is a branch of Dewsbury Pioneer's Industrial Society.

High Street, Hanging Heaton, looking uphill from near the post office. On the left is part of a trailer car from the Dewsbury, Batley & Birstall Tramways. This was purchased in 1905 by Erfus Bailey, plumber, and used as a storeroom near his house in High Street without proper planning permission. In November 1906, he was taken to court by Soothill Upper Urban District Council. Although Bailey was liable to a £5 fine, with a continuing penalty of £2 per day, the case was adjourned for a month to allow the defendant to remove or alter the structure.

Two
Birstall

Market Place, Birstall, c. 1910. The actual market had a chequered existence and never exceeded twenty-five stalls.

Market Place, Birstall. No. 1623

Market Place, Birstall, *c. 1920*. The erection of the statue on the left in 1912, to commemorate the life and work of Joseph Priestley, was the culmination of a plan to develop the Market Place, which lasted three decades. Birstall's growth during the nineteenth century derived from the discovery of local coal and the establishment of textile mills. With several famous people having been associated with the place, its current claim to eminence has little connection with industry. Amid much opposition from residents, who claimed that the town was capable of managing its own affairs, the Urban District of Birstall, including the hamlet of Howden Clough, was incorporated into the Borough of Batley on 1 April 1937.

Market Place, Birstall, *c.* 1910, with Bond Street beyond the lamp. At extreme right is the Lion Stores grocery shop. Their chain of stores appeared in several West Riding towns, some of them eventually operating under the name of J.W. Hillard Ltd. This company moved into the supermarket business.

Market Place, Birstall, *c.* 1910. To the left is the Wesleyan Methodist Sunday School in Chapel Lane.

Low Lane, Birstall, *c.* 1913. Occasionally called Market Street, Low Lane became the town centre's busiest thoroughfare, but the youngsters in this picture seem to be in no danger.

Low Lane, Birstall, *c.* 1920, looking the opposite way, with Middlegate behind.

Cambridge Road, Birstall, early 1930s. After the First World War, Birstall Urban District Council purchased 25 acres of land to the northwest of Church Street on which to erect council houses to ease its housing shortage. This area, which included Cambridge Road, became known as the Nova Estate. On the whole, the houses were well-built and stylish.

Coach and Six Hotel, Gelderd Road, Birstall. A sign on the building offers accommodation for cyclists and good stabling. The card was posted from the house with a cross to New York, USA, in August 1908. When demolished in 1955, the hostelry was claimed to be at least 300 years old.

Oakwell Hall, Birstall, *c.* 1907. This sixteenth-century Tudor manor house carries the date 1583 over a porch, but the building has been much altered since then. In Charlotte Bronte's novel, 'Shirley', it features as Fieldhead. The hall and grounds, which were taken over by Kirklees Council, now form the venue for many events.

Wellcroft Road, Howden Clough, *c.* 1925. James William Hudson, who published the card, kept the village post office and grocery store.

Three
Schools, Churches and Hospitals

Children's Flower Show, Gregory Street Council School, Lower Soothill, 1911. The annual event was organised by Soothill Flower Society, with several hundred children usually entering their display of mainly wild flowers. The shows were followed by tea, buns and games in a nearby field.

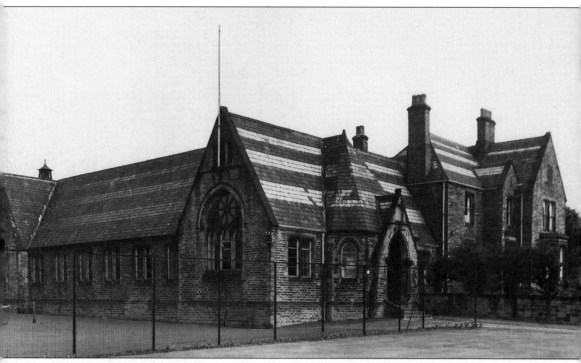

Boys' Grammar School, Batley, *c.* 1930. Replacing an earlier school founded in 1612, this school was erected at Carlinghow in 1878. It was enlarged and improved in 1913/14, when new classrooms were added. Other new facilities included lecture, geography and woodwork rooms, two science laboratories, a dining room and a gymnasium. The seven full-time and two part-time teachers received a proper staffroom. An area which had previously been sub-divided into classrooms was converted into an assembly hall. Pupils had previously assembled in a smaller lecture room, where the staff had customarily lined up behind the long demonstration bench in front, while the headmaster sat at the harmonium to play the hymn. Because the war intervened, the new facilities were not at first fully appreciated. Four members of staff were called to serve in the forces and temporary teachers stepped into the breach.

Girls' Grammar School, Batley, art class, 1909. The Higher Grade School for Girls was opened at Field Hill in 1894. It became the Girls' Grammar School in 1905, but closed in 1981, when pupils moved to Howden Clough. The earlier Batley Girls' Free School, near Blakeridge Mills, was closed in the 1870s.

Girls' Grammar School, gym class, 1909.

Girls' Grammar School, teachers, 1909. Back row, left to right: Misses Hollom, Evans, Risby, Martin. Front row, left to right: Misses Williams, Richards, Ellison, York, Law.

Girls' Grammar School, Batley, c. 1935.

Girls' Grammar School, library, *c.* 1935.

Girls' Grammar School, gymnasium, *c.* 1935. Compare with the earlier picture on page 45. The pupils' gear has been updated and the gym is properly equipped.

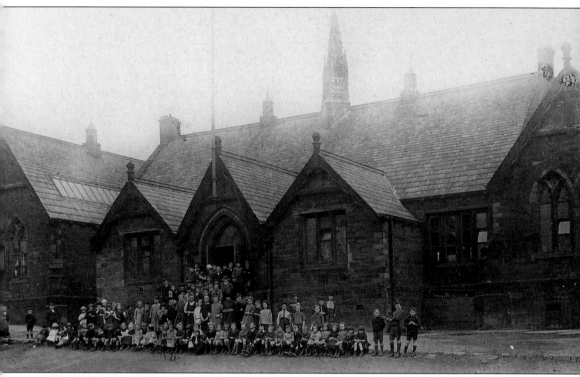

Christ Church School, Staincliffe, *c.* 1930. It was opened in 1869, one year before the Forster Education Act of 1870, which made elementary education compulsory, and required the setting up of local boards to provide enough schools. Previously, religious bodies had taken responsibility for providing some of the educational establishments.

Birstall National School, infants class, 1901. This Church of England school was opened on Kirkgate in 1818. It was enlarged in 1848, when a school house was added, and 1894.

Stocks Lane (Church Lane), Batley, c. 1906. The fifteenth century tower of All Saints' Parish Church, with overhanging battlements, peeps above the trees. Other parts of the church are even older, but it was extensively restored in 1873/4. Nearer the camera are the Parish Church School and School House, built in 1861/2. The school catered for children of all ages, but the infant department became separate in 1872. In 1936, a radiogram was bought for the school from the proceeds of a jumble sale and children selling jam jars.

All Saints' Parish Church, entrance to churchyard from Branch Road, c. 1910.

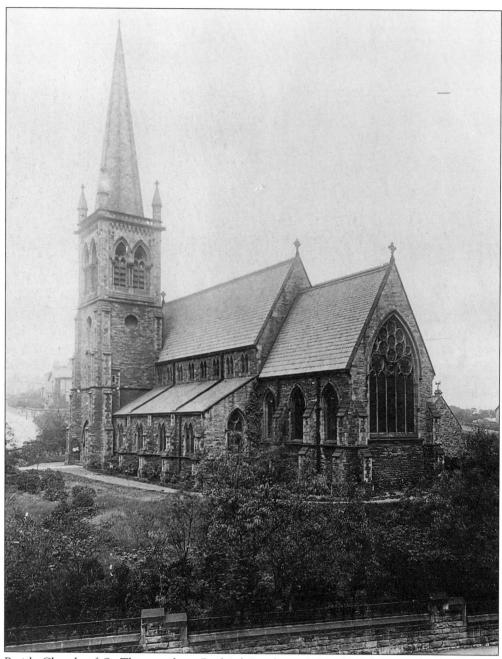

Parish Church of St Thomas, from Rutland Road, *c.* 1894. Grosvenor Road is in the left distance. The church, with a parsonage and school, was built in 1868 on a site given by the Earl of Wilton. It was one of several churches erected to meet the needs of an expanding industrial town.

Zion Chapel and Branch Road, Batley, c. 1908. John Wesley, the eighteenth-century Methodist founder, never intended to break away from the Anglican Church, but was barred from so many established buildings that the Wesleyan Methodist Church came into existence. Within the original Wesleyan Church, petty squabbles and doctrinal differences led to further divisions. As well as lesser bodies, the Primitive Methodist Church, the United Methodist Free Church and the Methodist New Connection were formed. In 1907, the latter two joined with the Bible Christians (also Methodist) to form the United Methodist Church. Long before then, the Baptists, Congregationalists and other Nonconformist bodies had created further divisions. In 1932, Methodist Union brought together most of the separate Methodist groups. After the Second World War, the size of many congregations started to diminish. In the 1850s, the Methodist New Connection, having held services at several locations in Batley, built a chapel at the top of Branch Road to seat 600 persons. In 1869, this was demolished and replaced by an even larger building called Zion. Having survived the unions of 1907 and 1932, it is now known as Central Methodist.

MORNING ATTENDANCE.

38	1st Sunday.	2nd Sunday.	3rd Sunday.	4th Sunday.	5th Sunday.
JANUARY					✳
FEBRUARY		✳			
MARCH		✳			
APRIL		✳			
MAY		✳			✳
JUNE	✳				
JULY	✳				
AUGUST					
SEPTEMBER					✳
OCTOBER					✳
NOVEMBER				O	
DECEMBER				●	

AFTERNOON ATTENDANCE.

38	1st Sunday.	2nd Sunday.	3rd Sunday.	4th Sunday.	5th Sunday.
JANUARY	✳		C		✳
FEBRUARY		✳		✳	
MARCH		✳		✳	
APRIL		✳		✳	
MAY		✳		✳	
JUNE	✳		✳		
JULY	✳		O		
AUGUST	✳		✳		✳
SEPTEMBER		✳		✳	
OCTOBER		✳		✳	
NOVEMBER	✳		✳		
DECEMBER	●				

The mark of a "✳" denotes EARLY attendance.
The mark of a "O" denotes LATE attendance, and counts one-half value.
The mark of a "●" denotes fifteen minutes late, and is of no value.

Should the Scholar be prevented from coming by illness, this Card, if brought to the School by a parent or any other responsible person, will have the early-mark affixed to that effect.

Attendance card. It belonged to W.H. Burnley who attended Zion Sunday School in 1897. The morning session commenced at 9.15; afternoon at 1.45. The school had four superintendents, two secretaries and various other teachers and helpers. Young Burnley was, it seems, an erratic attender and probably received no prize at the end of the year.

Chapels, Batley Cemetery, viewed from the lodge entrance, 1905. The two separate chapels, one for the Nonconformists (left) and one for the Church of England, further exemplified the discord which existed between the denominations.

Wesleyan Methodist Chapel, Hick Lane, Batley, *c.* 1912. This, the town's main Wesleyan Chapel, was opened in 1861. Its drab exterior belied its splendid interior. Closure came in the 1950s, when most of the congregation transferred to Zion.

Wesleyan Methodist Chapel, Cross Bank, Batley, *c.* 1908. The Sunday School building was opened on 18 February 1869; on the same day, the foundation stone for the chapel was laid. Its cost was borne by the Brearley family, in memory of Robert Brearley. He was the founder of Robert Brearley & Son Ltd, worsted manufacturers, Queen Street Mills, Bradford Road. The chapel was filled to overflowing for the opening on 21 March 1871.

Wellington Street worshippers. These bookmarks, with deckled (embossed) edges were produced in Lancashire, c. 1929, and probably sold to raise funds for the respective organisations. Batley Town Mission was situated in Wellington Street, near the Technical School. One of its longest serving missioners was James Gladwin, a vigorous exponent of the Christian cause. He died c. 1925. The Primitive Methodist Chapel and Sunday School were situated between Hume Street and Peel Street, but facing Wellington Street. The Primitives moved there in 1869 when they purchased Providence Independent Chapel, erected by the Congregationalists in 1839. Although the building possessed an internal gallery and seating for 600, it had a dour exterior and was said to be badly constructed. In 1844, the young men of the chapel dug out a room beneath the main building to form a Sunday school for teaching the Bible, and also reading and spelling. Some years after the Primitives took over, the chapel was severely damaged by fire. They constructed a better building with a school at the rear. The old Independent burial ground in front was retained.

Batley Castle Salvation Army band and Sir Ben Turner CBE, 1930s. Born in Holmfirth, Turner eventually moved to Batley. He joined the Independent Labour Party at its foundation in 1893. He became MP for Batley in 1922 and, after losing the seat, regained it in 1929. For twenty years, he was General President of the National Union of Textile Workers, and an active fighter for better working and living conditions.

Salvation Army songsters, 1930s. Their headquarters, known as Batley Castle, were in Branch Road, until they moved to purpose-built premises on Bradford Road.

Parish Church of St Paul, Hanging Heaton, *c.* 1905. The foundation stone was laid on 23 August 1823. A little over two years later, the church was consecrated by the Archbishop of York. The vicarage is visible just to the right of the church.

St Paul's Parish Church, Hanging Heaton. The photograph was taken before the 1916 fire, but after some alterations carried out in 1894, which included installation of the carved stone pulpit.

Christ Church, Vicarage and School, Staincliffe Hall Road, Staincliffe, c. 1905. The church was built in 1867; the church school and vicarage in 1869. Notice the degree of harmony in the design of the three buildings.

Parish Church of St Peter, Birstall, c. 1928. In 1865, the old church was found to be too dilapidated for restoration, partly due to collapse of old coal workings and burial vaults beneath the floor. It was decided to rebuild and enlarge at a cost of £18,000. The Wormald family were the largest donors, but rich and poor people subscribed according to their means. The church was reconsecrated on 29 April 1870 by the Bishop of Ripon.

John Nelson's study, Birstall, *c.* 1910. John Nelson was born in Birstall in 1707 and apprenticed to a stonemason. While working in London in his early married life, he came under the influence of John Wesley, founder of Methodism. Nelson became the object of ridicule from his workmates, whose hearts were said to be as hard as the stone in which they worked. Nelson returned to Birstall, studied the Bible and became a preacher. He spread the word in his home town and throughout the West Riding, often working in the open air. When John Wesley arrived in Birstall, he found not just a preacher but a whole society of Christians waiting to welcome him. With the founder's encouragement, Nelson preached in many parts of the land, even as far away as Cornwall. He was imprisoned in Halifax and Bradford and, as further punishment, impressed to serve in the army for three months. In his own town of Birstall, he was held in high esteem. John Nelson was serving in Leeds at the time of his death in 1774. Thousands of people joined in the funeral procession to Birstall, in striking contrast to the angry mobs of earlier days. In 1750, Nelson had helped as a mason in the building of a small chapel at Birstall. The picture shows his small study, erected in 1751 in the chapel yard. The high backed chair was used as an open-air pulpit, with a ledge at the back to support a Bible. The sundial, left, was made by Nelson in 1760.

Wesleyan Methodist Chapel, Birstall, *c.* 1909. It was erected in 1846 in what became known as Chapel Lane. To avoid confusion, it was later called St John's. The third hymn on the board, to precede the sermon, is Charles Wesley's 'O for a thousand tongues to sing.'

Wesleyan Sunday Schools, Birstall, *c.* 1913. These were erected near the chapel in 1886, and replaced an older school building. Partly because of declining attendance, the congregation of St John's Methodist moved to the Sunday School in 1968. The chapel, after becoming a listed building, was converted to office accommodation.

Harvest Festival, Mount Tabor Chapel, Birstall, 1909. In the middle of last century, large numbers of people broke away from the Wesleyan Methodist Church to form the Wesleyan Reform Union, because they objected to centralisation of power in the hands of a few leaders. After meeting in various buildings in Birstall, the Wesleyan Reformers built Mount Tabor at North Terrace in 1858. It closed in 1967 and was later demolished. The congregation amalgamated with St John's Methodist.

Batley & District Hospital.

THE THIRTY-FIRST ANNUAL

SUNDAY CONCERT,

(PRESIDENT - HIS WORSHIP THE MAYOR, D. STUBLEY, ESQ , J.P.)

IN AID OF THE ABOVE, WILL BE HELD IN THE

CRICKET, ATHLETIC, & FOOTBALL FIELD, BATLEY,

On SUNDAY, August 13th, 1911,

TO COMMENCE AT 2-45 p.m.

FULL BAND AND CHORUS OF 300 PERFORMERS.

Conductor - Mr. JOHN FEARNLEY.

Batley Old Band will play Selections,

AND WILL ALSO PLAY TO THE FIELD.

ALL ARE REQUESTED TO JOIN IN SINGING THE HYMNS.

The Committee appeal to the public for their generous support in aid of the above institution.

ADMISSION BY SILVER COLLECTION.

PROGRAMMES ONE PENNY EACH.   A. SYKES, *Hon. Sec.*

E. P. LOBLEY, HALIFAX ROAD, BATLEY.

Batley & District General Hospital, Carlinghow Hill. The foundation stone was laid on Easter Monday 1881. The buildings were opened on Easter Tuesday 1883 by the Earl of Wilton. Extensions and improvements were completed in 1908 and 1925. After closure in 1988, the hospital was converted to a private nursing home. As the above programme cover implies, concerts were one way of raising funds.

Batley & District General Hospital. This is the building shown on the previous page, when in use as a military hospital in 1918.

HERBERT SCHOFIELD, Magnetic Healer, Herbalist, and Masseur.

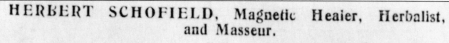

Sufferers from all kinds of diseases, no matter how long standing, made to walk after 20 years' suffering.

———o———

Testimonials can be seen.

———o———

Will visit at these Addresses :—

37, CROSS STREET, MORLEY,
Monday, Wednesday, and Friday, 10 to 12 and 2 to 9.

———o———

52, QUEEN STREET, BATLEY,
Tuesdays, 10 to 12, and 2 to 9;
Saturday, 3 to 7.

———o———

Thursdays and Saturdays.
Will visit Holbeck, Dewsbury, Earlsheaton, Ossett, or any other address if notified.

———o———

Thursday and Saturday private cases attended any distance

Residence—52, Queen Street, Batley.

Alternative medicine!

Four
Industry and Trade

Lower Soothill, looking north, c. 1905. In the foreground are the Batley Gasworks, with three gasholders. These were erected on land to the south of Grange Road. Soothill Wood Colliery is on the horizon, left, while Soothill Lane climbs away towards Woodkirk. At a meeting of Batley Town Council in June 1906, a recommendation from the Gas Committee that the town's lamplighters should have a week's holiday with pay each year was passed without opposition.

Industrial scene, c. 1907. Providence Mills are in the background. They were situated near the bottom of Branch Road. The round chimney appears to be a replacement for the lesser square one. In the foreground, on the opposite side of Bradford Road, is the yard of Batley Colliery, with coal carts and pit props.

Blakeridge Mills from Mayman Lane, *c.* 1908. They were owned by J.T. & J. Taylor Ltd. The initials stood for the brothers John, Thomas and Joshua. The complex was extended several times, new offices being added as late as 1923. The firm also owned Branch Road Mills and Cheapside Mills, and had a warehouse in Station Road, thus making it the largest woollen manufacturer in Batley. Most processes were carried out at the mills, from raw wool to finished cloth and, particularly in its early days, the firm was involved in rag grinding. A large part of the production was for the worldwide export market. Former Batley Grammar School pupil, Theodore Cooke Taylor, scholar, philanthropist and politician, was the company's most famous chairman. He died in 1952, aged 102.

G & J. STUBLEY LIMITED BATLEY Yorkshire

BOTTOMS
MILLS
BATLEY
YORKSHIRE

Also .
Hick Lane Mills, Batley
and
Calder Mills, Wakefield

London Office :
12 & 13, Bow Lane, E.C.
Cables, "Stubleys, Batley

Woollen Manufacturers to the Wholesale Trade only

Our Mills contain the latest and most up-to-date plant, and thus the fabrics are produced under the best of all conditions

His Majesty King George V. accompanied by Her Majesty Queen Mary, visited these Mills on July 10th, 1912

CONTRACTORS TO BRITISH AND ALLIED GOVERNMENTS

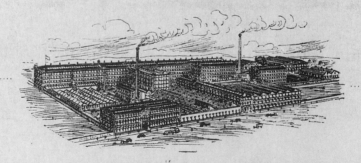

G. & J. Stubley Ltd, 1917 advertisement (previous page). It shows the company's Bottoms Mills, between Bradford Road and Mill Lane. Around 1830, George and James Stubley began their careers in a Batley mill, working from six in the morning to seven at night. After earning 1s 6d a week as pieceners, they eventually received 12s a week as fettlers. Losing their father, the brothers became family breadwinners, augmenting their earnings by working in their spare time. In 1850, they bought land in the Bottoms, near Batley Beck, and erected a building. After a period as commission spinners, they turned to the weaving of blankets and cloth. During the Crimean War of 1854/7, the brothers secured a large government contract to supply army blankets. Before its completion, the war ended and the contract was cancelled. This was the first of a series of ups and downs suffered by the firm. In the 1860s, the Stubley brothers focused their attention on the lucrative European market. A fire in 1866 destroyed some new premises in Mill Lane. Eight years later, the original structure in Bradford Road was burned down. But, with rebuilding and expansion, the business began to rank as one of the most enterprising in the Heavy Woollen District. It became a limited company in 1895. In time, the firm relied less on reprocessed wool and more on virgin wool. The range of products was immense. When the welfare of workers became a priority, whitewashed mill interiors were replaced with bright colours. A canteen was opened during the Second World War. This, and the distribution of tea and cakes from a trolley every afternoon, was a far cry from brewing tea from a steam heated tank in the mill yard.

Millworkers, c. 1910. They are posed in the yard of Ephraim Hirst & Co. Ltd, cotton spinners and doublers, Smithies Mill, Bradford Road, Birstall. Doubling was similar to spinning, but involved twisting two or more single yarns together to form a stronger thread.

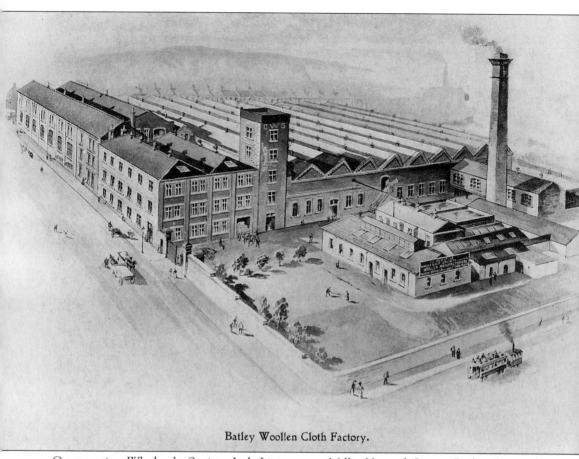

Batley Woollen Cloth Factory.

Co-operative Wholesale Society Ltd, Livingstone Mills, Howard Street, Batley Carr. The original mill was started in 1874 as a Workers' Productive Society. After a period of prosperity, it succumbed through a decline in trade and was taken over by the Co-operative Wholesale Society in 1886. The CWS added most of the buildings shown here, paying particular attention to the provision of light and air. At the mills, the society specialised in the weaving of high-quality woollen and worsted suiting material. The CWS abandoned its Livingstone Mills in 1961 to concentrate production elsewhere. The mills were taken over by Velmar Textiles Ltd for the manufacture of pile fabrics for rugs and soft furnishings. Velmar also took over the town's Greenhill Mills.

Co-operative Wholesale Society, Livingstone Mills, Batley Carr. The workers are assembled in the mill yard to celebrate (it is believed) the Silver Jubilee of King George V and Queen Mary. Observe the bunting, Union Jacks and fancy hats. At extreme left, in trilby, is Fred Asquith, who was born in 1878. He started as office boy in 1892 and became chief cashier. Next to him, wearing a bowler, is William Beaumont, who worked in the offices. For many years, the manager of the mills was Samuel Boothroyd, who was grandfather of Derek Boothroyd, author of the book *Nowt so Queer as Folk*. On his death, he was succeeded by Joseph Hirst, the man seated in front in bowler. His father, George, had been a designer at the mill. Also seated at the front, wearing glasses, is Fred Haigh, a tuner. In the long light-coloured coat towards the right is Clarence Gothard, warehouseman. The mill had its own brigade of volunteer firemen. The helmets, hatchets and other accoutrements were stored in a large glass case in one of the warehouses. The brigade appeared several times at the Manchester CWS Exhibition and won prizes.

Dorothy Lobley, later Mrs Greenwood, was born in 1909. Aged 14, she started working at Carrbrook Manufacturing Co., who were costume and underwear manufacturers at Carr Bridge Mills, Bradford Road, Batley Carr. She served a three-year apprenticeship, passing through most departments, but was then made redundant when the company went bankrupt. Dorothy obtained a job at Jessops (Tailors) Ltd, whose factory was in Station Road, Batley. Founded in 1854, the firm became the largest tailoring organisation in Batley and, via its range of shops in the West Riding, sold made-to-measure and ready-to-wear men's and boys' suits. Dorothy was a jacket lapel stitcher; using a small American sewing machine, she stitched pieces of canvas into the lapels to stiffen them. Although Dorothy spent most of her time stitching, she recalls going into other departments, including one which seemed like an oven because of the steam presses. In another department, steam was pumped through pipes into steam irons. At this time, Dorothy lived at 26 Mitchell Avenue, not far from the Shoulder of Mutton. To get to work, she walked along a footpath, down Upper Road and Town Street into Bradford Road, where she caught a tram to Hick Lane. After clocking-in, she worked from 8.00 a.m. until 5.45 p.m., with a break for dinner. Dorothy stayed at Jessops for about thirty years. Mitchell Avenue was part of a small estate of terrace houses, which included Robin Lane, North View Terrace and South View Terrace. The stone through-houses, built by Dewsbury Pioneers' Industrial Society, had cellars and yards. Each outside privy was shared between two homes. After Dorothy Lobley married Walter Greenwood, they went to live in a bungalow on West Park Street. Walter had a butchering shop in Town Street, Batley Carr. Mrs Greenwood eventually returned to live in a house in South View Terrace, owned by the Adams family. When, many years before, the Adams family had just moved into the area, their little son, Stanley, lost his way home. He was found by Dorothy and chaperoned back to anxious parents. This and other kindnesses were not forgotten, so when the house in South View Terrace became vacant, Mrs Greenwood took precedence. The photographs show Dorothy as a schoolgirl, left, and in her teens.

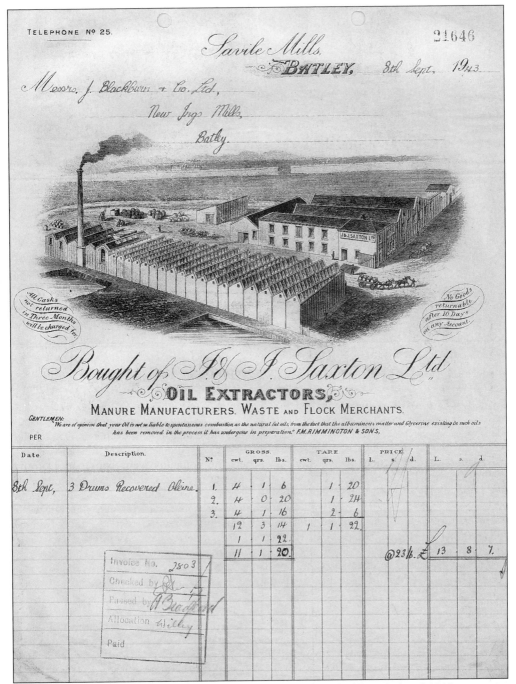

21646

Savile Mills,

BATLEY, 8th Sept, 1943.

Messrs. J. Blackburn & Co. Ltd.,

New Ings Mills,

Batley.

All Casks not returned in Three Months will be charged for.

No Goods returnable after 10 Days on any Account.

Bought of J. & J. Saxton Ltd

OIL EXTRACTORS,

MANURE MANUFACTURERS. WASTE AND FLOCK MERCHANTS.

GENTLEMEN: "We are of opinion that your Oil is not so liable to spontaneous combustion as the natural fat oils, from the fact that the albuminous matter and Glycerine existing in such oils has been removed in the process it has undergone in preparation." F.M.RIMMINGTON & SONS,

PER

Date.	Description.	No.	GROSS.			TARE.			PRICE			L.	s.	d.
			cwt.	qrs.	lbs.	cwt.	qrs.	lbs.	L.	s.	d.			
8th Sept.	3 Drums Recovered Oleine.	1.	4	1	6		1	20						
		2.	4	0	20		1	24						
		3.	4	1	16		2	6						
			12	3	14	1	1	22						
			1	1	22									
			11	1	20				@23/6.			13	8	7.

Invoice No. 2803

Checked by

Passed by A Bradford

Allocation Willey

Paid

J. & J. Saxton Ltd, Savile Mills, Alexandra Road. The billhead, although dated 1943, carries an engraving from around 1900. The company produced flocks, manure and oil from various woollen wastes. The oils, or oleines, were supplied for oiling rags to reduce breakage when converting to shoddy. Some of the poorer flocks were used for wallpapers.

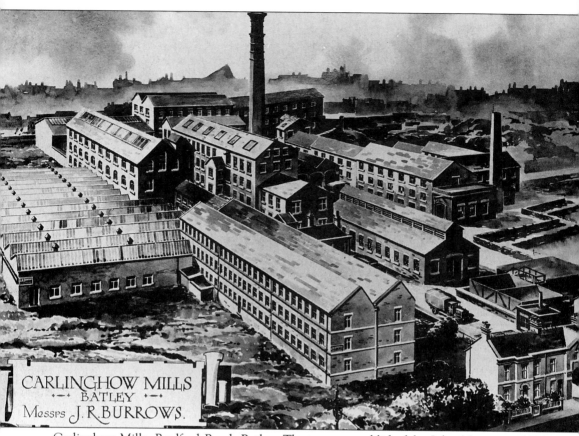

CARLINGHOW MILLS
•—• BATLEY •—•
Messrs J.R.BURROWS.

Carlinghow Mills, Bradford Road, Batley. These were established by John Nussey in 1826. Spinning and various connected processes were undertaken, but not weaving. Multi-storeyed buildings were added c. 1831, c. 1860 and c. 1875. Weaving sheds were built c. 1875. Carlinghow Mills were later owned by Brooke, Wilford & Co. Ltd, woollen manufacturers. In 1928, they offered the complex for sale by tender. It covered almost 8 acres, the floor area of the buildings being 17,000 square yards. Two Lancashire Boilers were included. One, made by J. & J. Horsfield of Dewsbury, was installed in 1893; the other, manufactured by Spurr Inman of Wakefield, arrived in 1909. Also included was a Green's Economiser. Carlinghow Mills were purchased by Messres J.R. Burrows for the sorting and storage of rags (the firm had originated in 1879). By supplying to the local shoddy and mungo trade, a historic Batley industry was kept alive. The firm acquired the nearby Victoria and Fountain Mills and formed two associate companies. One was Burkraft Ltd, which specialised in the wholesale of divans, mattresses, candlewicks etc. and now weaves rugs and blankets which are exported to several countries. The other, Shackletons (Carlinghow) Ltd, became famous for high-seat chairs. Following the decline of the woollen trade, the concern managed to survive into the 1970s, largely because of the two new companies. The 1980s saw the end of flock production. Bob Burrows, the company secretary, decided on a programme of site renewal, including the subdivision of the buildings into lettable units. Over forty tenants are now engaged in a range of trades and industries. The textile-related ones help to sustain a great tradition. The artists impression shows Carlinghow Mills, c. 1932. The entry from Bradford Road is in the lower right-hand corner. To the left are the weaving sheds; at extreme right is the mill reservoir. The two-bay multi-storey building in the centre foreground was erected in 1919. Part of it was taken over during the 1930s depression as an extra dole office, access being gained direct from Bradford Road via a bridge over Carlinghow Brook.

J.R. Burrows, Carlinghow Mills, *c.* 1930. The entrance block on Bradford Road, erected in 1877, is to the right of centre, behind the tram standard. Because the passage for pedestrians and vehicles was flanked by a small time office, right, and a cottage, left, which probably housed a night watchman, the entrance block controlled both day-time and night-time entry. A larger house stands adjacent to the cottage. Ten more mill cottages were situated to the rear of the mill complex. Part of Fountain Mills can be seen to the right. The line of Ford trucks includes three vehicles with double axles at the rear.

J.R. Burrows, Carlinghow Mills. This view from the entrance was sketched by A.E. Black in 1947.

J.R. Burrows, Carlinghow Mills. This 1947 sketch by A.E. Black shows the weaving sheds and the building erected in 1919.

J.R. Burrows, Carlinghow Mills, *c.* 1935. On the left is a smaller reservoir. Compare this photograph with the sketch at the top of the previous page.

J.R. Burrows, mixed vehicle fleet, *c.* 1950.

J.R. Burrows, Carlinghow Mills, rag sorting, *c.* 1932. By then, the stark conditions experienced by many workers in the cold, damp and badly lit buildings, which characterised the rag industry, were becoming a memory.

J.R. Burrows, Carlinghow Mills, rag warehouse, *c.* 1935. The distant man in the plus-fours is Frank Burrows, world champion roller skater, who frequently performed at the Batley rink.

Fire, Joseph Newsome & Sons, woollen manufacturers, Victoria Mills, Batley Carr, 4 October 1916. At 5.00 a.m. on Wednesday morning, smouldering bales were discovered in the mill yard by William Brown, who was checking that everything was in order for a 6 a.m. start. Suddenly the bales burst into flame, the fire quickly spreading to the main four-storey building. It was attended by Batley and Dewsbury Fire Brigades; also by firemen from Livingstone Mills. The devastated four-storey block is shown above; the lower picture shows debris in Bradford Road.

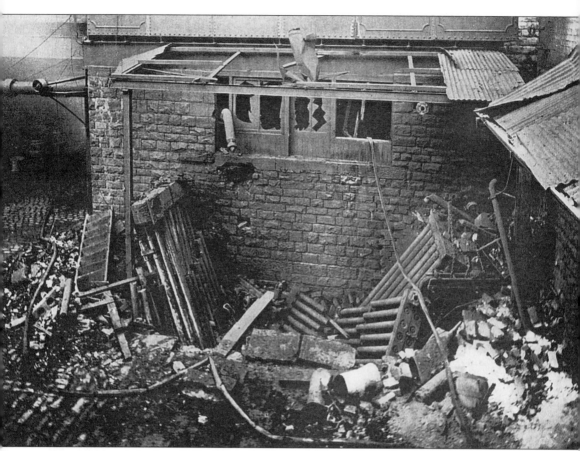

Economiser explosion, G.H. Hirst & Co. Ltd, woollen manufacturers, Alexandra Mills, Alexandra Road, Batley. The violent explosion occurred in the late afternoon of 29 July 1936. A volume of steam was seen issuing from the economiser, followed by a loud report, with steam and black smoke rising into the air as high as the top of the mill chimney. Most of the economiser and its tubes were completely shattered and the surrounding brickwork was demolished. In the neighbourhood of the explosion, everything was covered in soot and slime. Broken bricks and fragments of metal were blown in all directions. Miss Hilda Brooke, typist, who was seated near a window in an office about forty feet distant, was struck on the head with a piece of metal and killed. Also killed were the works' engineer, Walter Hey, and two boiler firemen, George William Ashton and Willie Land. Mr C. P. Tattersfield, director, who was also in the offices, was badly injured. Samuel Hemingway, labourer, who was on the steps of the economiser at the time of the explosion, was blown towards the engine house and severely scalded.

Fire brigade. The photograph is believed to have been taken in Batley, *c.* 1890, but the exact location is unknown.

E. Dixon, milk retailer, Batley Carr. Milk used to be taken round in churns by horse/pony and float, and ladled into the housewife's jug or basin, for storage in the cellar or pantry.

Batley miners' distress fund, 1920s. In Batley, the First World War was followed by years of economic difficulty. By 1921, 3,000 people in the town were out of work. Around three-quarters of these were textile workers; almost half the remainder were colliers and quarrymen. Families were reduced to picking coal from spoil heaps. The above striking miners toured the town with a street piano (tingalary) to collect money for wives and children. Note the dog on top.

Batley miners' distress fund. Four more striking miners pose beside the street piano. Both photographs were probably taken in the Wilton Street area. By the early 1940s, when no pits remained in Batley, local miners had to travel to Gomersal or Shaw Cross.

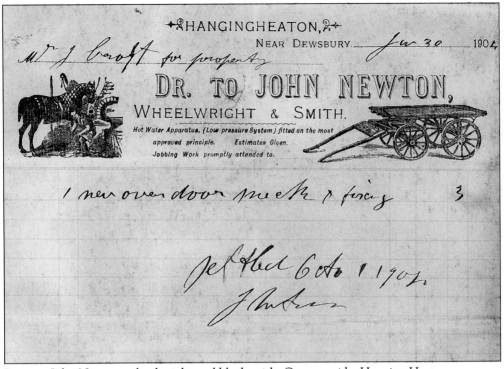

HANGINGHEATON,
NEAR DEWSBURY

Jan 30 ____ 1904

Mr J Croft for property

DR. TO JOHN NEWTON,
WHEELWRIGHT & SMITH.

Hot Water Apparatus, (Low pressure System) fitted on the most
approved principle.   Estimates Given.
Jobbing Work promptly attended to.

1 new oven door mesh & fixing   3

Settled Octr 1 1904

J Newton

Invoice, John Newton, wheelwright and blacksmith, Commonside, Hanging Heaton.

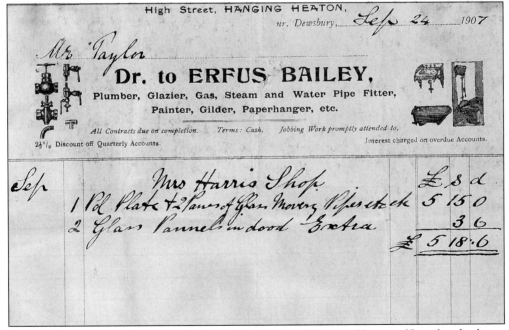

High Street, HANGING HEATON,
ur. Dewsbury, *Sep 24* ____ *1907*

Mr Taylor

Dr. to ERFUS BAILEY,
Plumber, Glazier, Gas, Steam and Water Pipe Fitter,
Painter, Gilder, Paperhanger, etc.

All Contracts due on completion.   Terms: Cash.   Jobbing Work promptly attended to.

2½% Discount off Quarterly Accounts.   Interest charged on overdue Accounts.

Sep	Mrs Harris Shop	£	s	d
	1 Pol Plate & 2 Panes of Glass Moverg Pipes etc etc	5	15	0
	2 Glass Pannels in door Extra		3	6
		£5	18	6

Invoice, Erfus Bailey, plumber and glazier, High Street, Hanging Heaton. (See also the lower
picture on page 36). The work detailed above was executed for Mrs Rebecca Harris, whose
grocery shop was on Commonside, Hanging Heaton.

Miss Gertrude Harrison, fancy draper, 119 Commercial Street, Batley, *c.* 1912. Observe the corsets in the side window.

A. Firth & Sons, newsagents and stationers, 121 Commercial Street, Batley, *c.* 1914. The window has a fine display of picture postcards, including some views of Batley.

Market Buildings, c. 1907. The address of George Senior Vero, gentlemen's outfitter, was 4 Market Place, hence the large digit above the name. R.E. Lloyd, at Staffordshire House, was a quality china and glass dealer.

F.W. Woolworth & Co. Ltd, Commercial Street, Batley, mid 1930s. The newly widened street attracted a number of new shopkeepers. The Woolworth store is shown shortly after construction. A bright new store was soon erected to its left for Leeds based tailors Montague Burton Ltd.

Isaac Waddingham, pastry cook and confectioner, Commercial Street. Both sides of a folding card, issued *c.* 1904, are shown.

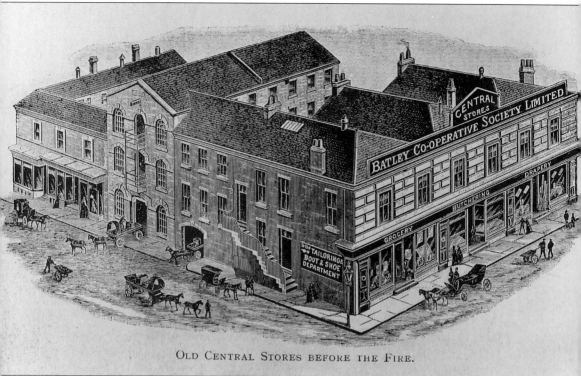

OLD CENTRAL STORES BEFORE THE FIRE.

Batley Co-operative Society Ltd, old central premises. This fraternity had its roots in the Batley Carr Equitable Pioneers' Society. Land was eventually purchased in Wilton Street, where three shops and a cottage were erected. Business continued to increase until, in 1867, members decided to sever the relationship and form the Batley Co-operative Society. In 1868, the society purchased land in Cross Bank on which to erect twenty cottages. In 1871, it was found necessary to alter and enlarge the premises in Wilton Street by buying a pair of shops and building a slaughterhouse. The society then had five distinct businesses – grocery, butchering, drapery, tailoring and footwear. A horse was purchased and a stable added. The departments were crowded with customers, men often accompanying their wives to carry home the week's provisions, knowing that, at the end of the quarter, they would receive a dividend from the profits. With further expansion in mind, various plots were considered for a new purpose-built store. The site on Commercial Street was chosen, where business would be transacted for the next hundred years. The building, shown above, was completed and ready for opening in 1873. In the early morning of 21 December 1901, a fire was discovered in the drapery department, which spread to the grocery warehouse. The former was completely gutted and the latter seriously affected. Much valuable stock was lost, although some of the departments, including the offices, suffered only water damage. Negotiations were opened with the insurance company and arrangements made for continuation of business with as little disruption as possible.

Batley Co-operative Society Ltd, new central premises, 1906. At the February 1902 quarterly meeting, members decided not to restore the old buildings, but to demolish and rebuild on the same site. For the duration of the rebuilding, contingency plans were put into operation. These included the acquisition of two empty shops nearby for grocery and butchering. It was also decided to disconnect the wholesale warehouse from the central stores and purchase a warehouse in Station Road. By early 1903, the various contracts for erecting the new central stores were let. Stonelaying demonstrations took place on 15 August 1903. These included a procession led by Batley Old Brass Band, the laying of memorial stones and a children's gala. On 8 December 1905, when building work was nearing completion, the grocery department was opened for business, but other departments had to wait a little longer. The formal opening of the whole building took place on Saturday 23 June 1906. To celebrate the event, a procession of officials and members, plus representatives of neighbouring Co-op societies, paraded the streets behind Batley Brass Band, before returning to the stores for the actual opening. Public teas were then served in the Congregational School, Town Hall and new Co-operative Hall. During most of the rebuilding period, a dividend of three shillings in the pound was maintained. The new building is shown above, prior to the fitting of the awning over the pavement.

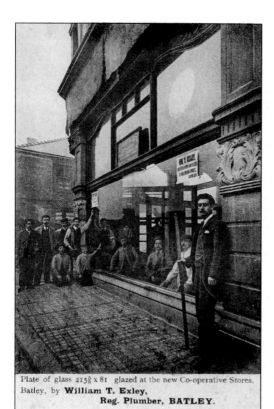

Plate of glass 215⅝ x 81 glazed at the new Co-operative Stores, Batley, by **William T. Exley**, **Reg. Plumber, BATLEY.**

Batley Co-op, 1905. William T. Exley, glazier and plumber of Commercial Street and Wellington Street, secured the contract for fitting this large plate of glass in the window of the drapery department.

Batley Co-operative Society Ltd, boot, shoe and tailoring departments, Commercial Street. These departments, previously located in Wilton Street, were opened on the south side of Commercial Street, near the main building, in April 1896. The property had been purchased a few years earlier. Workrooms for tailors and tailoresses were subsequently added on an upper floor.

Batley Co-op, No. 6 Branch, Bradford Road West. Branches were opened in many of Batley's suburbs, partly to fulfil the needs of people in new housing developments. This branch commenced business in April 1880. It was built on a plot of land leased from the Earl of Wilton.

Batley Co-op, No. 8 Branch, Healey. This was opened on Healey Lane in November 1884. Some competition was experienced, because the Heckmondwike & District Co-operative Society also opened a branch in the vicinity.

Batley Co-operative Society housing. The society branched into several spheres, such as the building of homes for members. The houses shown, known as Liberty Terrace, were built in Purlwell Hall Road, Mount Pleasant. Through a specially devised payment scheme, many tenants eventually became owners, and lived rent free.

Batley Co-op, boot repairing department, Wilton Street.

W. Roberts, watch dealer, Cross Bank. The postcard format price list shows a range of expensive and quality watches, plus some cheaper ones.

Nett Price List of "Limit" Watches.

GENT'S 7-JEWEL GRADE.
16 SIZE.

Style and Quality of Case.		Price each. £ s. d.
Gun Metal. Oxidized	Open Face...	0 12 6
Solid Nickel (White Through)	Open Face...	0 12 6
Silver, H.M., Light	Open Face...	1 2 6
„ „ Heavy	Open Face...	1 5 0
„ „	Hunting ...	1 6 0
„ „	Demi-hunting	1 10 0
10 Year Gold Filled	Open Face...	1 5 6
10 „ „ „	Hunting ...	1 7 0
10 „ „ „	Demi-hunting	1 14 0
20 „ „ „	Open Face...	2 2 0
20 „ „ „	Hunting ...	2 8 0
20 „ „ „	Demi-hunting	2 15 0
25 „ „ „	Open Face...	2 9 6
25 „ „ „	Hunting ...	2 14 0
25 „ „ „	Demi-hunting	3 1 0
9-ct. Gold Swing Ring Crystal	... ...	3 14 0
9-ct. „ Dome	Open Face...	5 4 0
9-ct. „	Hunting ...	6 4 6
9-ct. „	Demi-hunting	6 11 0
18-ct. „	Open Face...	12 2 0
18-ct. „	Hunting ...	15 13 0
18-ct. „	Demi-hunting	16 0 0

Extra for 15-Jewelled Movement,
each Watch ... **5/3**

Two years' Written Warranty with each Watch.

Sold by

W. ROBERTS,
4, North Bank Road,
Cross Bank,

The busy man consults his watch as often as his partner. The LIMIT can be relied on for true time

Limit Watches. This is the picture side of the above card, with some interesting office effects.

E. Swallow's greengrocery shop, *c.* 1912. It stood on Dark Lane in the Clerk Green area of Batley.

Miss Sarah Wood, grocer and confectioner, High Street, Birstall, *c.* 1905. The enamel signs advertise some now-vanished products.

E. Dickinson & Son, fruiterers and greengrocers, and fish, poultry and rabbit salesmen of Birstall, *c.* 1900.

E. Dickinson, Birstall, with his son and grandson, *c.* 1900.

Reprinted from the "Batley News," March 4th, 1939.

A. R. P. REFUGES MADE IN BATLEY

This exclusive "News" picture shows the first locally constructed A.R.P. steel shelter in the foundry of Messrs. A. J. Riley, the Batley boiler-makers.

Although similar to the models which may be issued to private householders, this design will be used primarily as an observation post in a mill or factory.

This shelter can be occupied by as many as four men, who, from the security of this welded steel beehive, can keep watch for injury or damage to valuable parts of the plant during an air-raid.

It can also be used to store valuable contracts, ledgers and plans during emergency.

3 Men type · 27-10 dd · ¼" plate ~ approx. 11cwt.

A.J. Riley and the Second World War (1939-45). Ration books were issued to everyone in January 1940. Sweets and bread were not rationed until 1942 and 1946 respectively, but tea, sugar, butter, meat and petrol were rationed from 1940 onwards. Eggs, cheese and clothes rationing started in 1941. Other contingency plans included the issuing of gas masks and construction of air raid shelters at homes and schools. The long-established firm of A.J. Riley & Son Ltd, of Victoria Works, Bradford Road, which was more accustomed to making boilers, tanks and condensers for the water, gas and chemical industries, started to manufacture an exclusive type of air raid shelter. Batley escaped lightly from enemy bombing, apart from some frightening events on the night of 12 November 1940, when high-explosive and incendiary bombs landed on mills and houses.

Five

Leisure

Cricket, Dewsbury v Batley, at Batley Cricket Field, 1912. From the left are Councillor J. Greenwood (Mayor of Batley) and Sir Mark and Lady Oldroyd of Dewsbury.

Rustic bridge, Wilton Park, Batley, 1911. The park was created out of 29 acres of land at Carlinghow Shays, which were given to the town by the Earl of Wilton. It was opened in 1910. A few of the park's new features are shown. Already a 'Please keep on the footpath' notice has appeared.

Mansion, Wilton Park, late 1920s. In 1909, the Victorian mansion and grounds known as Woodlands were purchased in auction for £5 by millowner Charles Robinson. He presented them to the Corporation for merging with the park. The Bagshaw Museum was established within the mansion by Walter Bagshaw JP, who was honorary curator until his death in 1927.

Lake, Wilton Park, *c*. 1938. It was constructed during the 1920s, with a central island for waterfowl. Bradford Road and few of Batley's mill chimneys provide the background.

Paddling pool, Wilton Park. This card, posted to America in July 1934, carries the message, 'I am spending a few days in Yorkshire with my uncle and cousin. At present, I am sat in the park. It is a lovely spot.' The tank on the hillside was presented by the War Office in 1919, in appreciation of the town's war savings efforts.

Bowling green, Wilton Park, *c.* 1935. The park took many years to lay out. The bowling greens and adjacent tennis courts were constructed in the 1920s, giving work to the town's unemployed.

Aviary, Wilton Park, 1921.

Refreshment rooms, Howley, *c.* 1906. Howley Hills, although not strictly within Batley township, provided a good day out, particularly at holiday times. The refreshment rooms were housed in the former gatehouse of Howley Hall.

Ruins of Howley Hall, *c.* 1906. The fine hall was completed in 1590 for Lord John Savile. It was besieged during the Civil War. Having passed to the Earl of Cardigan, much of the hall was blown up with gunpowder in 1730, because it was costly to maintain. The nearby farmhouse was constructed from the stone of the hall. It eventually housed the Howley Hall Golf Club. The golf course was enlarged in 1906, at which time the membership stood at 136 gentlemen and 55 ladies.

Railway Hotel, Birstall Smithies, *c.* 1908. Comic bands such as this relied as much on enthusiasm as musical ability.

Birstall Cricket Club, *c.* 1900. The photograph was probably taken at the cricket field on Leeds Road. E. Dickinson, a local greengrocer, is seated at front centre.

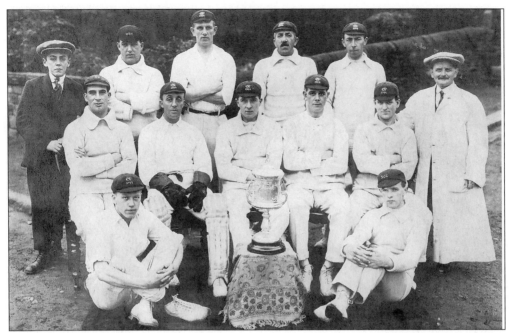

Soothill Cricket Club, 1914. The players are grouped at the junction of Gregory Street, left, and Soothill Lane, right, not far from the cricket ground.

Healey Cricket Club, at the ground in Healey Lane, probably early 1920s.

Roller Skating Rink, Bradford Road, Batley, *c.* 1910. This, the town's third rink, was opened in 1909. The staff and resident manager, A.M. St Clair, are shown. The building was also used for wrestling matches. It was destroyed by fire in May 1949.

Charabancs, Batley Market Place, *c.* 1905. Horse-drawn charabancs, which usually had seats which faced the front, were popular for day outings until the First World War. The exact nature of the happy event depicted here is unknown.

Soothill Wood, c. 1905. This favourite place for walking and playing was partly destroyed by the spoil heaps of Soothill Wood Colliery. Here, one boy climbs a tree while another holds a cricket bat.

Woodkirk Gardens. The message on the back of this card was written in the gardens on a Sunday afternoon in July 1910 and posted to Carlisle. 'It is splendid weather, and Rose has been showing us around as we have never been before.' The grounds were adjacent to the upper part of Soothill Wood (near the Babes in the Wood). It included a tea room, dance hall, swings, roundabouts, an aviary and small zoo. The site is now a housing estate.

Birstall Savage Club. It originated in 1884 as a men's social club for the pursuit of, 'Bowls, billiards, beef and beer, with a strong flavouring of solo whist, leavened with music and, of course, lots of politics.' The founder, and honorary secretary and treasurer until 1899, was James Francis Thomas Spiking, a Birstall insurance broker, pictured here *c.* 1904.

Birstall Savage Club. Summer excursions became a feature. On 28 June 1889, the party went to Helmsley, Rievaulx Abbey and Duncombe Park. Thomas George Simpson, flockmaker, and member of the club, took this photograph in Helmsley Market Place. From 1894 onwards, most of the trips lasted two days. On 26 and 27 June 1903, the excursion embraced Windermere, Keswick and Patterdale.

BIRSTALL SAVAGE CLUB.

ANNUAL MEETING February 5th, 1891, at 6-30 p.m.

Music Director—Mr. B. WILSON.

— PROGRAMME. —

Toast	..	..	"The Queen."	..	The PRESIDENT
Glee	..	..	"Here's life and health."	..	"The CHOIR"
Toast	..	..	"The President."	..	J. F. T. SPIKING
Song	..	..	"I'll conquer or die."	..	B. P. NETTLETON
Toast	..	..	"The Vice-Presidents."	..	F. A. SHEARD
Song	..	..	"The Gauntlet's down."	..	Dr. BROUGHTON
Toast	..	..	"The Secretary."	..	J. TALBOT
Glee	..	..	"Come where my love lies dreaming."		"The CHOIR"
Toast	..	..	"The rest of the Officers."	..	J. W. BLACKBURN
Song	..	..	"The Old Commodore."	..	G. WHITEHEAD
Toast	..	..	"The rest of the Members."	..	E. THURMAND
Song	..	..	"On the Banks of Allan Water."	..	J. TALBOT
Song	..	..	"I never interfere."	..	S. BOOTHROYD
Song	..	..	"Ever of thee."	..	J. W. BLACKBURN
Song	..	..	"McSauley's Twins."	..	W. THOMAS
Glee	..	..	"Brightest hopes are fleetest."	..	"The CHOIR"
Recitation	..	..	..	..	Dr. BROUGHTON
Song	..	..	"The Song that reached my heart."	..	B. P. NETTLETON
Song	..	..	"Mother Shipton."	..	S. MOWER
Song	..	..	"Swiss Châlet."	..	E. WISSLER
Song	..	..	"Bring back my Bonnie."	..	W. THOMAS
Song	..	..	"King Arthur."	..	E. THURMAND
Duet	..	..	..	..	BLACKBURN & NETTLETON
Song	..	..	"The Laughing Song."	..	S. BOOTHROYD
Song	..	..	"The Boys of the Old Brigade."	..	Dr. BROUGHTON
			&c.	&c.	

N.B.—No Billiard or Card Playing before 11 o'clock.

Birstall Savage Club. The society rented the club room and bowling green next to the Scotland Inn in Bradford Road, Birstall. In 1891, after their annual meeting, the members staged a musical evening, followed by dinner in the Scotland Inn. Part of the programme is reproduced here. Contributors included Benjamin Potter Nettleton and John William Blackburn, who were respectively an auctioneer and a shoddy manufacturer in Batley. In November 1891, Mrs Dean of Batley Station Hotel, presented Birstall Savage Club with 385 pieces of sheet music, a legacy from the defunct Batley Glee Party.

Temperance float, *c.* 1910. The temperance movement was strong in Batley, partly due to men like James Fearnsides, who started his own printing business and founded the *Batley News*. This decorated float may have emanated from the Temperance Hall in Brunswick Street. It won a first prize.

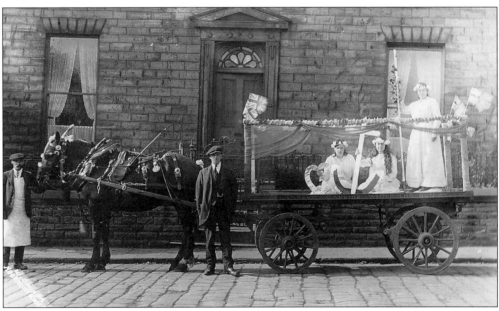

Decorated float, 1920s. The horse and rulley belonged to J. Lambert, carrier, of White Lee, Batley.

Six

Transport

Batley Railway Station, looking south, *c.* 1904. The station was shared by the London & North Western Railway and Great Northern Railway. These are the GNR buildings. To the left is the company's extensive goods yard.

Batley Station, looking north, *c.* 1904. 'Batley' appeared in the title of four local railway stations, which were Batley, Upper Batley, Batley Carr and Staincliffe & Batley Carr. Batley is the only station still in use. The London & North Western Railway opened the Leeds, Dewsbury & Manchester Railway in 1848 and gave Batley its first station. A line from Wrenthorpe Junction (which gave access to Wakefield) to Batley (via Chickenley Heath) was opened in stages by the Bradford, Wakefield & Leeds Railway from 1862 onwards, finally reaching Batley in 1864. This was absorbed by the GNR in 1865. That company's line from Batley to Dewsbury was opened in 1880. The GNR, anxious to obtain a firmer foothold in the Heavy Woollen District, constructed a line from Batley to join its Bradford-Ardsley line at Tingley. From there, a further section was built to connect with the Wakefield-Leeds line. It was opened throughout in 1890. Thus, although the LNWR controlled the direct line between Dewsbury, Batley and Leeds, the GNR broke the monopoly, albeit with some very heavily engineered lines. The two companies rubbed shoulders at Batley Station. In the above photograph, the LNWR buildings are on the left. Observe the subway which gave access to the other platforms. At extreme right are some of the GNR buildings. The different styles of architecture are apparent. The GNR opted for its familiar ridge-and-furrow canopies over the platforms. William Jubb, in his *History of the Shoddy Trade*, published in 1860, related how Batley Station was used for rag auction sales. 'On our arrival at Batley Station, we were struck with the vast quantity of rags, shoddy and mungo, heaped up on every hand. A large goods warehouse and a long shed were both filled with heavy bales. A considerable number of railway trucks were piled up with them, and a great number were also stacked on the ground, and covered with tarpaulin. We were informed that the great bulk of rags were from the Continent. About the time announced for the commencement of the sale, Mr Cullingworth, the auctioneer, accompanied by his assistants, drove up, and then, making his way to the lot intended to be sold first, he mounted upon the bale and stated what the lot was, referring purchasers to their catalogues. A circle of spirited bidders were soon formed around him, and in a short time – between two and three hours – there were sold 14 tons of rags and 300 bales of mungo. No time was wasted, and the only disturbance experienced arose from the shunting of railway trucks, some of them laden with huge blocks of stone, upon the sale ground.'

Upper Batley Station, looking south, *c.* 1910. The station, which opened in 1863, was closed in 1952. It was situated on the GNR line from Batley to Bradford (via Dudley Hill and Laisterdyke). Upper Batley Station served an elite suburb where wealthy manufacturers made their homes.

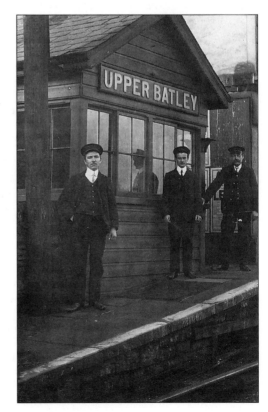

Upper Batley Signal Box, *c.* 1910. It is also visible on the previous picture. The level crossing adjacent to the cabin carried the road which led to Batley Hall.

Soothill Signal Box, *c.* 1910. Decorative bargeboards embellish the brick and timber GNR cabin. It is believed to have been located near Howley on the Batley-Woodkirk-Tingley line. It was probably demolished in the 1940s.

Upper Birstall Station, looking west, c. 1905. It was situated on the LNWR 'Leeds New Line' which provided an alternative route from Huddersfield to Leeds, via Spen Valley. Access to the all-timber station was from Gelderd Road. The left-hand platform, being built on an embankment, was supported on stilts. Closure came in 1951.

Norman Jackson, coal and coke merchant. The firm had premises on Station Road and, later, Bradford Road. The 20 ton steel railway wagon was supplied in the early 1930s by Charles Roberts of Horbury Junction.

Steam tram and trailer, early 1900s. The Dewsbury, Batley & Birstal (sic) Tramway Co. Ltd ran these combination units between Dewsbury, Batley, Birstall and Gomersal. Tram engine No. 7, new in 1881, and trailer car No. 14, new in 1898, stand outside the works of Pearson & Spurr Ltd, iron founders and power loom makers, in Bradford Road, Birstall. Unlike the trailer car shown on page 27, this trailer has one stairhead door at each end and probably transverse upstairs seating.

Tram terminus, Market Place, Batley, c. 1906. By late 1903, the steam trams were being replaced by electric trams. They reached the town centre via Upper Commercial Street but did not traverse Commercial Street. Above, Batley Corporation electric car No. 60, formerly No. 55, awaits departure for Heckmondwike. After the accidents shown on pages 114/15, car No. 55 exchanged numbers with single-deck car No. 60.

GREAT FLOOD. BATLEY CARR. MAY 25ᵗʰ 1925'ᵗ

Electric tramcars. Batley Corporation wanted to operate its own electric tramway, but realised that such a system would probably have to form part of a larger network. Having obtained a Board of Trade licence, it started to lay track within the town and ordered eight tramcars. The British Electric Traction Co. Ltd, which was planning to operate trams in much of the Heavy Woollen District, including Batley, unsuccessfully contested the matter through Parliament. Commonsense eventually prevailed, neither party claiming an absolute victory. The Yorkshire (Woollen District) Electric Tramways Ltd, which was part of British Electric Traction, agreed to run trams in Batley where the Corporation wanted them. The Batley cars were leased to the YWD and numbered into their fleet. They were painted green and cream instead of the YWD crimson and cream. The Corporation secured the right to sell power from its electricity station for all trams working in or passing through Batley. Electric tram services commenced in Batley on 26 October 1903. Conversion of the steam tramway was delayed, a full electric service between Dewsbury and Gomersal not commencing until 23 November 1905. The photograph shows YWD and Batley Corporation cars in 1925. Nearest the camera is an unnumbered YWD tram of the batch numbered 7-48, in near final form, with a top cover and solid panels around the balconies. Behind it is Batley Corporation tram No. 51, one of the eight originally open-topped cars with numbers 49-56. Notice the deeper waist panel on the Batley car. The single-decker is part of a YWD batch numbered 70-81, which were bought from Sheffield Corporation in 1919/20. At the end of the line is YWD car No. 8.

Tram accident, 16 January 1904. Batley Corporation car No. 55 ran out of control while descending Thorncliffe Road and crashed through a wall at the junction with Track Road. The driver and two passengers were injured. Hyrstlands Hall is behind the trees on the right.

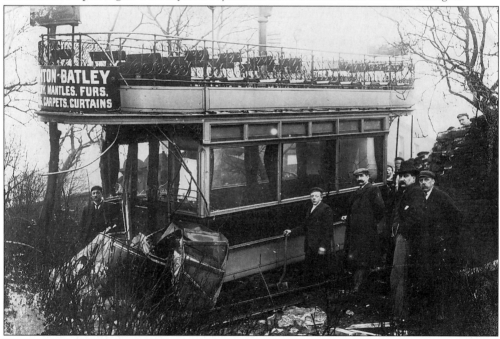

Tram accident, 16 January 1904. Crashed car No. 55 is shown from the opposite side. At official investigations, blame was attached to the driver who probably approached the corner too fast and failed to correctly apply the brakes.

Tram accident, 29 August 1904. Tramcar No. 55 had a further mishap while rounding a corner near the New Inn in Purlwell Lane. The car, having got out of control, ran into a horse-drawn van belonging to George Parrott, confectioner, of Commercial Street. Its driver, J.W. Corrison, was delivering pastries to Mr Driffield's eating house, right. There were no serious injuries.

Miss G. Elsie Taylor, Mayor of Batley. Very briefly she became a tram driver. When the last YWD car, No. 11, ran along the sole remaining route (from Dewsbury to Cleckheaton via Halifax Road) on Wednesday 31 October 1934, she took over the controls at the Batley boundary and drove it to the Heckmondwike boundary.

Decorated tramcar, probably late 1920s. It is either No. 55 or 61 in the YWD fleet. These two single-deck cars were created by joining pairs of shorter cars together, initially for use on the busy Dewsbury-Ravensthorpe service.

Bus Station, Batley, from Bradford Road, c. 1965. At extreme left is the Masonic Hall. Next to it is the former Empire Cinema, which closed in 1961.

Seven
Events and Disasters

'Ye Olde Village Wedding', Congregational Church, Birstall, 22 November 1913. The imaginary wedding was followed by numerous individual items to raise money. The bride, groom and cake occupy the centre of this picture.

Coronation of King George V and Queen Mary, 22 June 1911. Local events included parades, parties, decorations and a bonfire. This floral arch was erected near the eastern end of Commercial Street. It is viewed looking towards Hick Lane.

Coronation of King George V and Queen Mary, Town Hall decorations, 22 June 1911.

Flood, Bradford Road, Batley, 9 June 1910. The front of Stubley's Bottoms Mills is visible to right of centre. This road, which runs along the valley of Batley Beck, was, until recent improvements, liable to flooding. The man who wrote 'Very nice weather over here' on the back of this card was being sarcastic.

Flood, Bradford Road, Batley Carr, 25 May 1925. The workmen on the truck seem happy. Miss Edith Brown, owner of the tobacconist shop, left, looks to be marooned.

Visit of King George V and Queen Mary to Batley, 10 July 1912. On the eventful day, their Majesties, having visited Dewsbury, arrived at Stubley's Bottoms Mills where they were greeted by the chairman, Mr David Stubley, who was also Mayor of Batley. The royal couple were escorted round the mill to the acclaim of assembled workers. At 4.45 p.m., the King and Queen were driven up Hick Lane and Commercial Street to a crowded Market Square, where a platform with red baize, shown above, had been erected in front of the Town Hall. As their Majesties alighted from the car, children sang the National Anthem. The royal couple mounted the platform on which civic dignitaries and their wives were already seated. The Mayor spoke and the King replied. According to a local report, the proceedings lasted three minutes, after which their Majesties were whisked away to Heckmondwike.

Visit of King George V and Queen Mary to Batley, 10 July 1912. Their Majesties, having left their car, stand on the platform in front of the Town Hall. Some children on the left managed to secure an elevated position. Many of the 4,000 schoolchildren who attended, particularly the smaller ones, were sad because they never saw the royal pair. Parents and teachers were indignant.

Visit of the Duke and Duchess of York to Batley, 24 April 1928.

Birstall Co-op children's gala procession, 27 July 1907.

Coronation Festival, Birstall, 1911. The 'King' and 'Queen' are J. Crabtree and F. Ratcliffe. The National School is on the left.

DR PRIESTLEY MEMORIAL UNVEILED, 19/11/12.
BIRSTALL.

Unveiling of Joseph Priestley Memorial, Birstall. Joseph Priestley was born at Fieldhead, Birstall, on 13 March 1733. He probably attended Batley Boys' Grammar School. He later studied at Daventry Academy. In his search for truth, Priestley had a varied career. He became a dissenting parson at Needham Market in 1755 and Nantwich in 1758. For six years from 1767, he was minister at Mill Hill Unitarian chapel, Leeds. He was librarian to Lord Selborne from 1773 to 1780. During this period, Priestley revolutionised the study of chemistry by isolating several gases, including oxygen and ammonia. His radical views and actions led to his fleeing to America for safety. He died there in 1804. It took over a century for the people of Birstall to honour their famous scientist and philosopher. The statue, at the edge of the Market Place, was unveiled by notable scientist, Sir Edward Thorpe, on 19 November 1912. The photograph was taken shortly after. Perhaps one of these children grew up to be a famous scientist.

Hanging Heaton Church Fire,
(Hartley) Feb. 17th, 1916. (Dewsbury)

Fire, St Paul's Parish Church, Hanging Heaton, 17 February 1916. At 4 o'clock on Thursday morning, Samuel Pleasants, of Quarry Street, saw a glare from his bedroom window, which seemed to be coming from Hanging Heaton Church. After dressing, he ran to knock up the verger, J.R. Sykes, of High Street. Pleasants then ran to Show Cross Post Office and phoned for the fire brigade. The verger found the whole church interior well alight, with flames leaping through the roof. Dewsbury Fire Brigade was soon in attendance, but Batley Fire Brigade was delayed in Grange Road because the toll bar gate was closed. By 7.00 a.m., the fire was under control. The communion plate and some of the parish registers were rescued. Most of the church interior was destroyed, including the wooden gallery and two-manual organ. The roof collapsed; only the walls and tower remained. The west end of the church is shown after the fire. Some of the people who gathered talked of German incendiaries as a possible cause.

Fire, St Paul's Parish Church, Hanging Heaton, 17 February 1916. The probable cause was a flash of lightning. A thunderstorm had occurred in the middle of the night. A former plan to erect a lightning conductor, following lightning damage to one of the tower's pinnacles some years earlier, had been postponed.

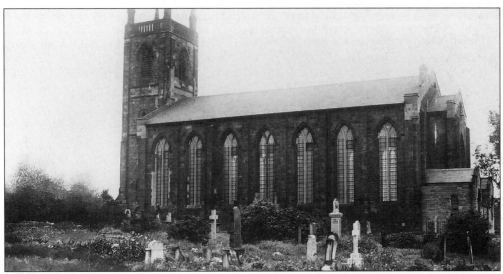

Parish Church, Hanging Heaton, *c*. 1934. The lighter-coloured new stonework of the restored building is noticeable.

Soothill Upper War Memorial.

Unveiling of Hanging Heaton (Soothill Upper) War Memorial. 4 September 1920. Four years after the fire, the church is still without its roof.

Unveiling of Hanging Heaton War Memorial, floral tributes.

Peace Pageant, 19 July 1919. Mid July was chosen by the nation for special peace celebrations. In Batley, these were spread over several days and included a gala at Mount Pleasant, a firework display at Field Hill and street decorations. Here, the Saturday procession passes Preston Jenkinson's carpet shop at Hick Lane crossroads. Observe the ice cream man.

William James Ineson, Mayor of Batley, 1907/08. He lived at Ivy Mount, Ebury Street, and attended Zion Chapel. A believer in self-education, he wrote to Andrew Carnegie in 1902 for a donation towards erecting the Public Library.

Hanging Heaton Carnival, 27 June 1925. The procession, headed by Dewsbury Brass Band, started from the Railway Hotel, Commonside. Some of the 500 people taking part are shown, with Ravensthorpe Comic Band on the right. After the parade, everyone repaired to a field off Crackenedge for refreshments and sports. Apart from a fancy dress parade with prizes, a feature of the 1925 event was a competition for the best decorated street or terrace. It was won by Bromley Street.

Funeral, Commercial Street, c. 1905. The cortege approaches the front of Zion Chapel. Identity of the deceased is unknown.